# WARSHIPS ILLUSTRATED No 11

**1.** HMS *Springer*, seen here on the Mersey on 27 July 1945, was one of the five 'S' Class boats built under the 1943 Programme. These submarines had the same basic dimensions as the previous boats but carried a Mk. XII 4in gun mounted in a semi-enclosed position integral with the conning tower structure; the external stern torpedo tube was omitted, to reduce top weight. Note the raised mast for the Type 291 search radar. *Springer* was transferred to the Israeli Navy in 1958 and renamed *Tanin*. (IWM FXL. 7316)

⚓ WARSHIPS ILLUSTRATED No II

# BRITISH SUBMARINES
## in World War Two
### PAUL J. KEMP

a&ap

ARMS AND ARMOUR PRESS

# Introduction

First published in Great Britain in 1987 by Arms and Armour Press Ltd., Link House, West Street, Poole, Dorset BH15 1LL.

Distributed in the USA by Sterling Publishing Co. Inc., 2 Park Avenue, New York, NY 10016.

Distributed in Australia by Capricorn Link (Australia) Pty. Ltd., P.O. Box 665, Lane Cove, New South Wales 2066.

British Library Cataloguing in Publication data:
Kemp, Paul J.
British submarines in World War Two.—(Warships illustrated; 11).
1. Great Britain. *Royal Navy* 2. World War, 1939–1945—Naval operations, British 3. World War, 1939–1945—Naval operations—Submarine
I. Title II. Series
940.54'51 D784.G7

ISBN 0-85368-778-1

Edited and designed by Roger Chesneau; typeset by Typesetters (Birmingham) Ltd., printed and bound in Great Britain by The Bath Press, Avon.

Prints credited to the Imperial War Museum are for sale on application to its Department of Photographs, Lambeth Road, London SE1. The Visitors' Room is open to the public by appointment.

◄2
2. HMS *Seraph* returns to Portsmouth on 24 November 1943 after service in the Mediterranean. As operations in the Mediterranean declined after the capitulation of Italy the 'S' and 'U' Class submarines, which had borne the brunt of the fighting, were either brought home for refit or ordered to the Far East. (IWM A.21104)

The British have traditionally had a record of public distaste for submarines and submarine warfare. In various interwar disarmament conferences British politicians sought to secure the abolition of the submarine, and during both World Wars stories of German U-boat atrocities formed a principal element in British propaganda. It is, therefore, somewhat ironic that during the Second World War British submarines were, for a time, the only weapon which could be used to really hurt the Axis powers.

At the outbreak of the Second World War Britain had 58 such vessels available, most of which were of modern construction. During the interwar period British submarines were built with a view to quality rather than quantity, and the soundness of this approach was later demonstrated when boats designed during the 1930s were built in large numbers and were able to absorb various wartime modifications without affecting the basic design. Some of these boats gave useful service well into the postwar era.

The type of war fought by British submarines was very different from that conducted by the German U-boats in the Atlantic or by American submarines in the Pacific. On the whole, British submarines worked in shallow waters strewn with minefields and close to enemy bases with their concentrations of anti-submarine forces. Targets were few and were invariably heavily escorted. Given these circumstances, the successes achieved by British submarines are remarkable. In home waters their activities formed the only redeeming feature of the Norwegian campaign and for the rest of the war German capital ships in Norwegian waters could only move under heavy escort. The Mediterranean, with its clear and shallow water, was not the ideal environment for underwater operations, but it was here that British submarines had their most important influence on the war. Operating from Malta, despite the bombing, as well as Alexandria and Gibraltar, they savaged Rommel's supply convoys and prevented the adequate reinforcement of German and Italian forces in North Africa at the time of the Battle of El Alamein. Significant successes were also scored against Italian warships, and the Italian fleet became severely restricted in its movements. Submarine operations in the Far East had to wait until forces could be spared from the Mediterranean and home waters, but from 1943 British boats were increasingly active in this theatre.

From 1939 to 1945 British submarines sank 493 enemy merchant ships totalling 1,524,000grt and damaged another 109 ships (518,000grt); to these figures must be added the 35 enemy merchant ships destroyed by mines laid by submarines. Results against enemy warships were equally satisfactory: six cruisers, sixteen destroyers, 35 submarines and 112 other warships were sunk, whilst two battleships, ten cruisers, two destroyers, six submarines and 35 other warships were damaged. Another six enemy warships were destroyed by submarine-laid mines.

The price of these successes was high. Seventy-five British submarines did not return from patrol – approximately 35 per cent of the 215 boats that served in the Royal Navy during the Second World War – and 3,142 submariners lost their lives while another 360 became prisoners of war (out of approximately 25,000 men in Submarine Command). Winston Churchill paid eloquent tribute to the work of Submarine Command when he said, 'Of all branches of men in the Forces, there is none which shows more devotion and faces grimmer perils than the submariner . . . Great deeds are done in the air and on land, nevertheless nothing surpasses your exploits'.

The photographs in this book are principally from the extensive collection at the Imperial War Museum in London, and I am grateful to that institution for permission to reproduce them. I am also grateful to Gus Britton of the Royal Navy Submarine Museum, to David Webb and to David Hill for their assistance.

Paul J. Kemp

▲3  ▼4

3. *L26* was one of three 'L' Class submarines remaining in service with the Royal Navy at the outbreak of war. These boats were a saddle tank design, descendants of the 'E' Class which had served with distinction in the First World War, but by 1939 they were obsolete. *L26* is shown here without her 4in gun during boom defence trials at Rosyth in 1942. All three boats were sent to Canada for training duties in 1944, *L26* being expended as a target on 25 September 1945. (IWM A.9399)

4. *H43* was built by Armstrong, Walker, to a modified American design in 1919. In September 1939 nine 'H' Class submarines were left in service and, although they were obsolete, the shortage of new boats meant they were used on operations. In 1939–40 *H43*, together with her sister-ship *H33*, was used on covert operations to determine whether U-boats were harbouring in Irish territorial

waters. No evidence was found to indicate that U-boats were infringing Irish neutrality and the patrols were discontinued in mid-1940. (Wright and Logan)

5. *Oberon*, seen here at Spithead on 21 January 1943 after a refit in Portsmouth Dockyard, was the first British submarine to be designed after the First World War. The ending of the Anglo-Japanese Alliance in 1922 meant that the Royal Navy had to build submarines for long-range operations in the Far East, and *Oberon* measured 270ft overall × 28ft × 13ft and displaced 1,311 tons surfaced and 1,831 tons submerged. She was dogged throughout her career by mechanical unreliability and spent only a few months on operations at the beginning of the war before being relegated to training duties. Note the position for a 20mm Oerlikon gun worked into the after end of the conning tower. (IWM FL.3186)

▲ 6

**6.** HMS *Oxley* was one of two submarines completed for the Royal Australian Navy and handed over to the Royal Navy in 1931; the two boats were almost identical to *Oberon* except for the ram-shaped bow. *Oxley* was the first British submarine to be lost in the Second World War when she was torpedoed in error by HMS *Triton* on the night of 10 September 1939. She was out of her patrol position and failed to reply to three challenges and a recognition grenade fired by *Triton*. The commanding officer and one seaman were the only survivors. (IWM FL.3198)

**7.** *Otway*, the other of the two 'O' Class boats for the RAN, under way in April 1944. During the war she was originally employed in the Mediterranean before being recalled to home waters. She was scrapped at Inverkeithing in August 1945. (IWM FL.3194)

▼ 7

**8.** *Odin* at Hong Kong in 1940; note the tall W/T mast, which was essential for radio communications in eastern waters. *Odin* was built at Chatham Dockyard in 1928. At the beginning of the Second World War she remained in the Far East before being transferred to the Mediterranean where, on 14 June 1940, she was sunk by the Italian destroyers *Strale* and *Baleno* in the Gulf of Taranto – the first British submarine to be lost in the Mediterranean. (IWM FL.3191)

**9.** HMS *Olympus* taking on fuel oil in Manoel Creek, Malta, January 1942. On arrival in the Mediterranean *Olympus* had to be refitted at Malta because of her poor mechanical condition. In all the 'O' boats, and in the succeeding 'P' and 'R' Classes, the fuel tanks were located outside the pressure hull, an unsatisfactory arrangement since the light plating leaked, leaving a tell-tale oil stain in the water. *Olympus* was mined on 8 May 1942 while on passage from Malta to Gibraltar. The submarine was carrying a large number of additional personnel, including the crews of two 'U' Class submarines, because of the withdrawal of the 10th Submarine Flotilla from Malta. There were only nine survivors. (IWM A.6928)

▲10  ▼11

12▲

13▲

10. Members of the ship's company of *Osiris*, complete with mascot, on the casing at Beirut on 15 April 1943 after their return from patrol. On 22 September 1940 *Osiris* sank the Italian destroyer *Palestro* off Brindisi. The submarine survived the punishing conditions of the Mediterranean and was transferred to the Eastern theatre as a training vessel before broken up at Durban in September 1946. (IWM A.18071)

11. HMS *Phoenix* off Hong Kong in 1939. The six submarines of the 'P' Class were almost identical to the 'O' Class and therefore suffered from the same problems; the one major difference was that the shape of the bow was the same as *Oberon*'s. *Phoenix* was built in 1929 by Cammell Laird and was lost in the Mediterranean on 16 July 1940, probably as a result of a depth charge attack by the Italian torpedo-boat *Albatros*. (Author's Collection)

12. *Pandora*, one of four 'P' Class boats built by Vickers at Barrow, shown as completed in 1930. While serving in the Mediterranean *Pandora* and her sister-ship *Parthian* were modified to act as transport submarines to take supplies to Malta, their spare torpedoes and one of the battery banks being removed and some of the ballast tanks being adapted to carry petrol. *Pandora* made several voyages to Malta carrying supplies and RAF personnel, but after arriving at the island on 31 March 1942 she received two direct hits during an air raid on 1 April and sank before her cargo could be unloaded. (Author's Collection)

13. HMS *Parthian* at Beirut in January 1943. Under the command of Lt. Cdr. 'Bim' Rimmington, this boat scored Submarine Command's first success in the Mediterranean when she sank the Italian submarine *Diamante* off Tobruk on 20 June 1940. *Parthian* had a distinguished career in the Mediterranean but was presumed mined in the southern Adriatic in August 1943. (IWM A.14912)

**14.** The control room of the submarine *Proteus*. Behind the hydroplane operators stands the first lieutenant, responsible for the 'trim' (the way the submarine floats in the water in relation to her fore/aft line). *Proteus*, together with her sister-ships and the boats of the 'O' and 'R' Classes, had an operational diving depth of 300ft; the designed depth was 500ft. (IWM A.12503)

**15,16.** *Proteus* (photograph 15) was the most successful of the 'P' Class, as is suggested by the 'Jolly Roger' displayed by some of the crew (photograph 16) on their return to England on 30 October

1943. On 8 February 1942 the boat made an unsuccessful attack on what the captain had identified as a U-boat. The torpedoes missed and *Proteus* attempted to ram the 'submarine', only to find that it was the Italian torpedo boat *Sagittario*. As *Proteus* sheered away she lost her port foreplane, which tore a gash in *Sagittario*'s side. Ironically many of *Proteus*' complement were later drafted to the submarine *Tally-Ho*, in which they were to have a similar experience at the hands of a Japanese warship in the Malacca Strait. (IWM A.12506/IWM A.12499)

▲17

▲18　▼19

20▲

7. While the six units of the 'P' Class were under construction the
Admiralty ordered a further class of six, the 'R' Class, of which only
four units were launched, all in 1930. This photograph shows
*Regulus* in 1932. In appearance the 'Rs' differed from the 'Ps' in that
the 4in gun occupied a lower position and lacked the protective
shield fitted in the 'Ps' (although *Regent* and *Regulus* were
completed with the full shield and later modified). At the beginning
of the Second World War *Regulus* was with the 4th Submarine
Flotilla in the Far East. Eventually she was ordered to the
Mediterranean where she was lost in December 1940. (Wright and
Logan)

8. HMS *Regent* was built in 1930 by Vickers; she is shown here on
patrol in mid-Atlantic, January 1942. Note the difference in the
position of the 4in gun compared with the submarines of the 'P'
Class. *Regent* was mined in the Otranto Strait on 16 April 1943.
(IWM A.7356)

9. HMS *Rover*, built in 1930 by Vickers, was the only member of
the 'R' Class to survive the war. The 'Rs', together with the 'O' and
'P' Classes, were large submarines for which the confined waters of
the Mediterranean were not the ideal operating environment.
(Wright and Logan)

10. In the 1929 Programme the Royal Navy decided to revert to the
construction of fleet submarines, i.e. those designed to operate with
a battle fleet. The first unit was *Thames*, built in 1932 by Vickers.
With a displacement of 2,165 tons surfaced and 2,680 tons
submerged, *Thames* represented a considerable increase in size over
the 'O', 'P' and 'R' Classes, although she had a very low weight-to-
armament ratio since in order to fit the two 5,000hp, ten-cylinder
diesels required for high surface speeds the after torpedo tubes had
to be omitted from the design, thus reducing the armament to six
fixed bow tubes. On trials *Thames* made 21.5kts, which was an
impressive performance for a diesel boat of the period. It had been
intended to build twenty of these submarines, but the Admiralty
finally realised that the concept of the fleet submarine was obsolete
and the programme was abandoned. *Thames* was mined off Norway
on 23 July 1940. (IWM HU.2367)

21. *Thames* had two sister-ships, *Severn* and *Clyde*, which differed
slightly in appearance and were 1kt faster. This photograph, taken
from the cruiser *Hermione*, shows *Clyde* early in 1942. On 20 June
1940 *Clyde* torpedoed the battlecruiser *Gneisenau* off the Norwegian
coast, putting the German ship out of action for many months.
*Clyde* and *Severn* were transferred to the Mediterranean in 1941 and
to the Pacific in 1944, where their qualities of speed and endurance
could be put to better use. *Clyde* had to be cannibalized for spares
for *Severn* and was eventually broken up at Durban in July 1946.
(IWM A.7339)

21▼

▲ 22    ▼ 23

**22.** HMS *Porpoise*, built in 1932 by Vickers, was the first of a class of six submarine minelayers built between 1932 and 1938. The design derived from the experience gained with the minelaying submarine *M3* and the boats were slightly smaller than the *Thames* class though had many similar features. This 1935 photograph of *Porpoise* shows clearly the break in the casing forward of the conning tower which distinguishes this particular submarine from the others in the class. On 17 January 1945 *Porpoise* was attacked by Japanese aircraft in the Malacca Strait and, it is believed, was later sunk by Japanese ASW craft, thus becoming the 75th and last British submarine to be lost during the Second World War. (Wright and Logan)

**23.** This 1937 photograph of *Grampus* shows the considerable height of the casing necessary for the stowage of the boat's 50 mines; note also how the periscope standards have been offset to starboard to allow the mine casing to run the full length of the boat. *Grampus*, which was built at Chatham Dockyard, was depth-charged to destruction off Augusta on 24 June 1940 by the Italian torpedo boats *Circe* and *Clio*. (Wright and Logan)

**24.** *Narwhal* loading mines, possibly at Immingham, in 1940 shortly before she was reported missing off Norway. The mines were not stored in vertical tubes but in the long, high casing above the pressure hull. Inside the casing the mines, which were of the Mk. XVI self-mooring type, were laid on a rail fitted to the top of the pressure hull and were winched to the stern by a chain mechanism, to be launched from the hatch visible in the photograph. (IWM HU.45250)

**25.** The launch of *Seal*, the last of the six minelaying boats to be built, on 27 September 1938 at the Royal Dockyard at Chatham. When war broke out a year later *Seal* was on her way out to join the 4th Submarine Flotilla at Hong Kong but was recalled to home waters where she participated in operations off the Norwegian coast. Note the size of the hull: with a full load of mines the displacement of these boats was 1,810 tons on the surface and 2,155 tons submerged. (Author's Collection)

24 ▲    25 ▼

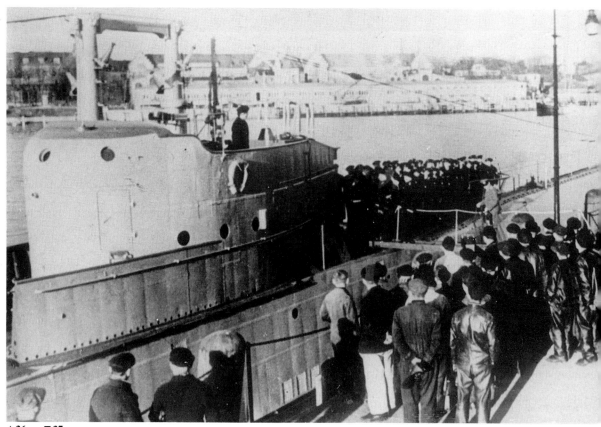

▲26    ▼27

**26.** In May 1940 *Seal* was ordered to lay a minefield in the Kattegat, but during the operation she was badly damaged aft by the explosion of a German mine and was only brought to the surface after herculean efforts by her crew. Her captain attempted to steer for neutral Sweden but after his boat was attacked by German aircraft, and in the face of approaching ASW craft and with his crew still suffering the effects of carbon dioxide poisoning, he took the difficult decision to surrender – a decision that was upheld by the Admiralty after the war. This photograph shows *Seal* being commissioned as *U-B* into the *Kriegsmarine* at Kiel. The Germans had high hopes for their prize but, as if in revenge, *Seal* never lived up to her new owners' expectations and she was scuttled in May 1945. (Author's Collection)

**27.** *Rorqual*, seen here in Sliema Creek, Malta, in February 1943, was the most successful of her class, laying a total of 1,284 mines (out of the 2,599 mines laid by the class as a whole); she was also the only one to survive the war. *Rorqual* participated in the 'magic carpet' operations to bring supplies to Malta, and also made good use of her gun. On one occasion in the Northern Adriatic she surfaced and with her 4in gun engaged a tug towing a battery of field artillery on a lighter. The lighter was damaged and the tug left in a sinking condition. (IWM A.14683)

**28.** As well as their outfit of mines the *Porpoise* Class were equipped with six 21in torpedo tubes in the bow; this photograph shows four of *Rorqual*'s tubes. Note the safety forks from torpedoes which found a target hanging on the bulkhead: one of them commemorates the sinking of the Italian submarine *Pier Capponi* south of Stromboli on 31 March 1941. (IWM E.5909)

**29.** Cramped conditions in *Rorqual*'s seamen's messdeck. The minelaying submarines carried a complement of 59, which included the specialist ratings required for minelaying operations. Note the bunks folded back against the bulkhead to provide more room. (IWM E.5918)

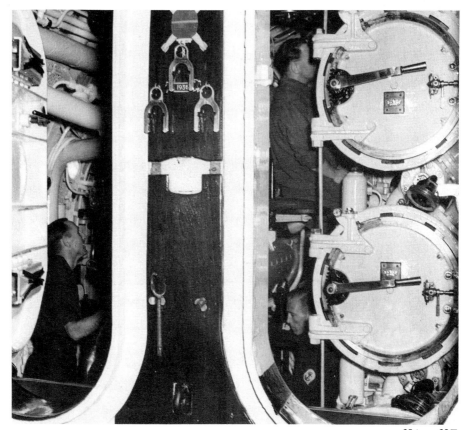

28▲  29▼

▲ 30

▲ 31    ▼ 32

**30.** HMS *Seahorse* was built at HM Dockyard, Chatham, in 1932 and was one of the first of 62 'S' Class submarines to be constructed for the Royal Navy between 1931 and 1945 and intended for operations in the restricted waters of the North Sea and Mediterranean. Great importance was placed on mechanical reliability, a quick diving time (20–30 seconds) and underwater manoeuvrability. *Seahorse* displaced 640 tons surfaced and 927 tons submerged and carried an armament of six 21in torpedo tubes, all in the bow, and a 3in deck gun (yet to be fitted when this photograph was taken). *Seahorse* was lost, probably mined, in the North Sea about 29–30 December 1939. (IWM FL.3449)

**31.** An early photograph of *Swordfish* showing the 3in gun on the hinged mounting with which two of the first four 'S' boats were fitted. The mounting folded down into the extension forward of the conning tower but it was later removed (because it created too much top weight) and replaced with a fixed deck mounting. (Author's Collection)

**32.** A photograph of *Sturgeon* surfacing in January–February 1943 when the submarine was acting as an ASW target at Mers-el-Kebir. This boat was loaned to the Royal Netherlands Navy between 1943 and 1945 and renamed *Zeehond*; she was broken up in 1947 after being returned to Britain. (IWM A.14360)

**33.** HMS *Salmon* was one of the *Shark* Class built between 1934 and 1937; the second group of eight boats were slightly larger than the first but carried the same armament. Note the 3in gun on the deck mounting and the extension forward of the conning tower forming the access hatch for the crew to man the gun and for ammunition to be passed up from the magazine. *Salmon* scored one of the earliest submarine successes of the war by damaging the German cruisers *Leipzig* and *Nürnberg* on 13 December 1939. Earlier, on 4 December, she had sunk *U36*, and on 12 December had been in a favourable position to intercept the homeward-bound German liner *Bremen* but was kept down by patrolling aircraft. *Salmon* was mined off Norway on 9 July 1940. (Author's Collection)

33▼

▲ 34 ▼ 35

**36 ▲**

**34.** *Shark* on completion in 1935. For the 'S' and subsequent classes the Admiralty abandoned the practice of placing the fuel tanks outside the pressure hull, thereby ending the problem of leaks which had so beset the 'O', 'P' and 'R' Classes. (Author's Collection)

**35.** On 5 July 1940 *Shark*, on patrol in the Skaggerak, was attacked by aircraft using depth charges. The submarine was unable to dive and was subjected to severe harassment, during which three members of her crew were killed and eighteen wounded. For five hours *Shark*'s crew beat off the attackers, but the long hours of daylight were against them. The commanding officer, Lt. Peter Buckley RN, prepared to scuttle the submarine while German minesweeping trawlers took off the crew (as shown in the photograph). *Shark* foundered as the Germans attempted to take her in tow. (IWM A.30697)

**36.** An interesting photograph of *Sealion* in December 1942 when she was operating as a training submarine with the 7th Submarine Flotilla at Rothesay. Note what appears to be a Vickers machine gun mounted aft of the conning tower to provide extra AA defence; *Sealion* and *Seawolf* were the only two boats to carry this weapon. (IWM FL.3306)

**37.** *Saracen*, built by Cammell Laird in 1942 and seen here entering Algiers harbour in February 1943, was one of the five 'S' Class submarines built under the 1939 War Programme. She was an improved version of the boats of the second group and was fitted with an external torpedo tube aft, giving a much-needed stern salvo. While working up in the North Sea *Saracen* sank *U-335*, and later, in the Mediterranean, she sank the Italian submarine *Granito*. On 14 August 1943 *Saracen* was herself sunk after a depth-charge attack by the Italian corvettes *Minerva* and *Euterpe*. (IWM A.16000)

**37 ▼**

▲ 38     ▼ 39

**38.** *Satyr* was another of the 1939 Programme 'S' Class. This photograph of her in Holy Loch on 26 January 1943 shows clearly the opening for the external stern torpedo tube and also a 20mm Oerlikon which has been added to the after end of the conning tower. *Satyr* was later converted to serve as a high-speed target and was broken up in 1962. (IWM A.14073)

**39.** An Italian schooner burns after being shelled by *Safari* in the Gulf of Poliocastro off the Italian coast in January 1943. *Safari*'s war service under the command of Cdr. Ben Bryant is well known, and during her subsequent service, under the command of Lt. R. B. Lakin, the boat wrought havoc among Italian coastal shipping prior to the invasion of Sicily. (IWM AX.159B)

**40.** *Safari* returns to Portsmouth from the Mediterranean, 8 September 1943. She has not yet been fitted with the stern torpedo tube. After a refit at Troon to prepare the boat for service in the Far East, *Safari* was instead assigned to the 7th Flotilla for training duties. (IWM A.19067)

**40▼**

▲41 ▼42

**41.** *Sickle* comes alongside the depot ship *Maidstone* at Algiers, April 1943. On 21 May 1943 *Sickle* sank *U303* but in June 1944 was presumed mined in the Antikithera Channel. (IWM A.16831)

**42.** *Stubborn* returns to Greenock on 25 February 1944 alongside the Norwegian warship *Narvik*. On 11 February *Stubborn* had attacked a German convoy off the Norwegian coast and had been heavily depth-charged. Two days later she attacked another convoy and had over seventy depth charges dropped on her; she was badly damaged but evaded her attackers, and in a daring rescue operation British destroyers ventured to within 23 miles of the Norwegian coast to tow the crippled submarine back to Holy Loch. (IWM A.21951)

**43.** The bridge of HMS *Stubborn*. The after periscope standard houses the attack periscope while the forward one is for the larger search periscope; the engine room telegraphs can be seen on the forward side of the attack periscope housing. *Stubborn*'s captain, Lt. A. A. Duff DSC RN, is second from the right. (IWM A.21952)

**44.** *Seraph*'s 'Jolly Roger' testifies to a distinguished record in the Mediterranean. This submarine participated in a number of special operations (as shown by the daggers on the flag), including the transport of General Mark Clark of the US Army to a covert meeting with French generals in North Africa before Operation 'Torch'. *Seraph* was later involved in the operation to deceive the Germans about Allied plans for the invasion of Sicily, featured in the book *The Man Who Never Was*. (IWM A.21109)

**45.** *Seraph*'s 3in gun crew after their return to Britain. The gun proved to be a most useful weapon for submarines operating in the Mediterranean and, later, in the Far East, where many of the targets were not worth the expenditure of a torpedo. (IWM A.21111)

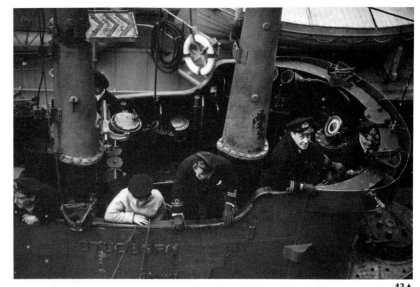

43▲

44▲   45▼

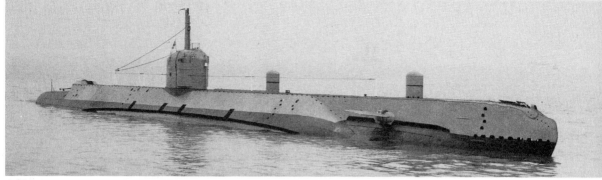

▲ 46

▲ 47

**46.** In July–September 1944 *Seraph* was converted to a high-speed target submarine for training warships in anti-submarine techniques. The reported construction of high-speed submarines by the Germans meant that ASW training needed to be carried out at greater speeds, which a conventional submarine with all the impedimenta of guns, periscope standards, etc. could not produce. In all, five 'S' Class submarines were selected for conversion. Compare this 1953 photograph of *Seraph* with that featured on page 4 of this book. (IWM FL.3584)

**47.** HMS *Stratagem*, seen here on 20 February 1944, was ordered to the Far East on completion and was sunk on 22 November the same year in the southern part of the Malacca Strait. After torpedoing a 2,000-ton merchant ship, the submarine was fiercely depth-charged by a Japanese destroyer, which caused severe flooding. Ten men escaped from forward and eight were picked up by the destroyer; only three men survived Japanese captivity, the others being executed or dying as a result of the conditions. (IWM A.21917)

**48.** HMS *Storm* returns to Portsmouth, 8 April 1945. From 1943 all new 'S' Class submarines were ordered for service in the Far East once activities in the Mediterranean theatre had quietened down. To give the submarines the extra endurance required for the long voyages between bases and patrol billets, two of the main ballast tanks were converted to carry fuel oil, thus increasing the total load from 45 to 67 tons; further conversion work on the ballast tanks meant that another 25 tons could be accommodated. (IWM A.28125)

**49.** The 'fore ends' on board *Storm*. This compartment combined the roles of workshop store, torpedo stowage and accommodation for some of her complement of 48. Conditions were very crowded, and after visiting an American submarine *Storm*'s commanding officer commented, 'I felt downright ashamed of the conditions in which some of my own seamen and stokers had to live'. (IWM A.28123)

▼ 48

49▶

0, 51. HMS *Shakespeare*, built by Vickers in 1941 and seen here at lgiers early in 1943, had one of the most harrowing experiences of ny British submarine during the Second World War. In 1944 she as transferred to the Far East and on 3 January 1945 was badly amaged in an engagement with a Japanese freighter and ASW essel off Port Blair following which her pressure hull was holed and he was unable to dive. Luckily she was able to creep away on the urface, but as she made her slow way back to Ceylon she endured 5 Japanese air attacks as her crew laboured to repair the damage. Vith her wireless out of action, *Shakespeare* headed for the patrol illet of her sister-ship *Stygian*, and on 6 January the latter was ghted and was able to radio for assistance; two days later the rippled submarine returned to Ceylon. Photo 51 shows *hakespeare*'s commanding officer, Lt. D. Swanston RN, and first eutenant, Lt. J. Lutley RN, inspecting damage to the starboard

side of the conning tower. (IWM A.16328/IWM A.27360)
52. HMS *Statesman*'s 3in gun crew on deck in the Far East, with the results of their handiwork burning behind them. This boat was one of the most successful British submarines in gunnery attacks on enemy shipping, with 49 vessels sunk and over 1,200 rounds of ammunition expended. (IWM AXA.152A)
53. *Sea Devil* (seen here on the Clyde in April 1945), *Scotsman* and *Scythian* differed from the other boats of the 1941 Programme in that they carried a 4in QF Mk. XII gun instead of the 3in weapon. The extra weight of this gun meant that the external after torpedo tube had to be omitted. Note the Type 138 asdic dome at the end of the after casing. These three submarines were the forerunners of the 'S' Class of the 1942/43 Programmes discussed later. (IWM FL.2256)

▲ 54 ▼ 55 ▼ 56

. A 21in Mk. VIII torpedo
ing loaded on board *Sceptre* at
ly Loch, September 1943.
e Mk. VIII was carried by all
itish submarines from the 'O'
ass onwards. The principal
rtime variant was the Mk.
II**, which weighed 3,245lb
d was 21ft 7in long. The
rhead originally comprised
2lb of TNT but was later
laced with one of 805lb of
rpex. The weapon had a
ge of 5,000yds at 45½kts
d 7,000yds at 41kts. Postwar
riants of this weapon are still
service with the Royal Navy,
years after the appearance of
prototype. (IWM A.18296)
. The 'Fruit Machine', an
ctrically driven mechanical
e control computer for the
pedo armament.
aditionally worked by the
urth Officer, this machine,
en fed with the target's
nge, course and speed,
gether with those of the
acking submarine,
termined the amount of DA
rector angle) or 'aim-off'
quired to hit the target. This
pe of machine was common to
British submarines of the
cond World War. (IWM
22331)
. The torpedo firing panel in
'S' Class submarine. The
rpedoes were launched from
e tube by means of
mpressed air; the AIV
itomatic inboard vent) drew
e compressed air into an open
nk after the torpedo had left
e tube, thus preventing the air
m escaping and giving the
acking submarine's position
ay. The empty tube then
ed with water, compensating
the weight of the torpedo
ich had just been fired and
eserving trim. (IWM
22332)
. A view of the 20mm
rlikon gun on board *Spiteful*
Scapa Flow, November 1943.
e Oerlikon was not a
rticularly satisfactory weapon
submarine service since it
s prone to frequent jamming,
t the weapon did provide a
easure of AA defence and in
stern waters was useful for
ooting up junks and other
astal craft. *Spiteful* was
nsferred to France in 1951–
and renamed *Sirène*, serving
th the French Navy until
68. (IWM A.20508)

57 ▶

**58.** Only three boats of the 1942/43 Programmes were completed with a 3in gun and a stern tube: this photograph shows *Sturdy* in January 1944, the other two being *Stygian* and *Subtle*. *Sturdy* and *Stygian* were the only two boats of the 1942/43 Programmes to have riveted hulls: all the other boats in this group were of welded construction and so had an increased diving depth of 350ft (Author's Collection)

**59.** *Selene* under way on the Mersey, July 1944. On completion *Selene* joined the 8th Submarine Flotilla in the Far East, based at Subic Bay, and participated in X-craft operations. (IWM FL.3454)

◀ 58       ▼ 59

▲ 60

**60.** HMS *Triton* was the first of the 'T' Class, which were built as ocean-going submarines to complement the 'S' Class. The design was of the saddle tank type, with a displacement of 1,330 tons surfaced and 1,585 tons submerged and a maximum operational diving depth of 300ft. The 'Ts' were armed with six internal bow torpedo tubes, plus two external tubes fitted in the bulge in the upper part of the bow and two more external tubes fitted to fire ahead on either side of the conning tower. This armament thus ga▨ a bow salvo of ten torpedoes, which was considered sufficient to d▨ with targets travelling at high speeds and at long range. A 4in Mk. XII gun completed the armament. *Triton* was lost in December 19▨ in the southern Adriatic, possibly as a result of an attack by the Italian torpedo boats *Altair* and *Andromeda*. (IWM FXL.10077)

▼ 61

1. HMS *Sentinel*, launched in July 1945, was one of only two boats (the other being *Seneschal*) of the 1942 group to be built by Scotts; the remainder were all built by Cammell Laird. *Sentinel*, together with *Seneschal*, *Spearhead* and *Sanguine*, were armed with the heavier Mk. XXII 4in gun instead of the Mk. XII fitted in the other boats. *Sentinel* was the last of the 'S' Class submarines to be built and was broken up in 1962; of the 62 boats in the class, eighteen were lost in action. (IWM FL.2261)

62. *Selene* was later converted to a high-speed target (or 'Slippery S') on the same lines as *Seraph*; she is shown here in December 1953. *Solent* and *Sleuth* of the 1942/43 group were likewise converted. (IWM FL.3455)

▲ 63

▲ 64    ▼ 65

3. *Triumph*, built in 1938 by Vickers, had [on]e of the luckiest escapes of any British [su]bmarine. On 26 December 1939 she [st]ruck a mine in the North Sea and lost [ei]ghteen feet from her bows. Mercifully [he]r torpedoes did not explode, thus [pr]oving the efficiency of their contact [pi]stols. *Triumph* was lost, cause unknown, [in] the Aegean in December 1941. (IWM [F]U.50)

4. HMS *Thetis* beached at Moelfre Bay, [A]nglesey, after her salvage following one [of] the greatest tragedies to befall the [su]bmarine service. While on her [ac]ceptance dive in Liverpool Bay on 1 [Ju]ne 1939 the boat proved 'reluctant', and [th]e order was given to check whether Nos. [5] and 6 tubes were filled with water as was [in]dicated on the trim statement. A [co]mbination of negligence by one of sub-[co]ntractors and sheer bad luck meant that [it] was not realized that the bow cap of No. [6] tube was open, and when the rear door [w]as opened the inrush of water could not [b]e contained. The submarine sank with [10]4 men on board; only four escaped. [I]WM FL.2039)

5. *Thetis* was raised, renamed *[T]hunderbolt*, and recommissioned under [th]e command of Lt. C. B. Crouch. On her [fi]rst war patrol she sank the Italian [su]bmarine *Tarantini* in a difficult stern-on [at]tack, and she later took part in the [ch]ariot attack on Palermo harbour in [w]hich the cruiser *Ulpio Traiano* was sunk [o]n 3 January 1943. It seemed that ghost of *[T]hetis* had finally been laid to rest, but *[T]hunderbolt*'s luck ran out on 14 March [1]943 when she was depth-charged to [d]estruction by the Italian corvette *Cigogna* [o]ff the north-west coast of Sicily. The [p]hotograph shows *Thunderbolt* in January [1]941. Note that the two external bow tubes [h]ave been removed; only *Thunderbolt* and *[T]riumph* received this modification. (IWM [A].2577)

6. *Thunderbolt* fires a practice torpedo [fr]om her starboard midships external tube, [M]alta, 15 February 1943. Later boats of [th]e 'T' Class had the two midships external [t]ubes facing aft which, combined with a [fi]fth external tube worked into the after [c]asing, provided a much needed stern [sa]lvo. Note also the platform for the 20mm [O]erlikon fitted to *Thunderbolt* during a [re]fit in 1942. (IWM A.14631)

7. A rare photograph of HMS *Triad*, [ta]ken in Mastrie Fjord in November 1939. [W]hile on patrol off the Norwegian coast *[T]riad* suffered a broken hydroplane shaft [ou]tside the hull and became [un]manageable. She was towed into the [fj]ord by the destroyers *Maori* and *Inglefield* [an]d later moved to Stavanger for repairs. [T]he Norwegian government waived the [c]ountry's rights as a neutral state under the [H]ague Convention and allowed *Triad* to [r]emain for longer than the permitted 24 [h]ours until repairs were completed. (IWM [H]U.51765)

8. A photograph of *Torbay* in Plymouth [S]ound in November 1942, showing how [th]e early 'T' Class boats were extensively [m]odified to meet the demands of the [S]econd World War. Note the 20mm [O]erlikon platform, the external stern tube [w]orked into the after casing and the Type [2]91 radar aerial at the after end of the [c]onning tower. (IWM FL.3438)

66 ▲

67 ▲    68 ▼

**▲69**

**69.** HMS *Trident* returns from patrol to her base at Holy Loch, 19 March 1942. On 23 February 1942, under the command of Cdr. G. M. Sladen, *Trident* blew the stern off the German cruiser *Prinz Eugen* near Trondheim. Built in 1938 by Cammell Laird, *Trident* was broken up in 1946 at Newport. (IWM A.7934)

**70.** A weather-beaten HMS *Truant* returns to Holy Loch, 3 December 1942. In the early part of the war *Truant* served in home waters, where she torpedoed the German cruiser *Karlsruhe* on 9 April 1940. Under the command of Lt. Cdr. H. A. V. Haggard RN. *Truant* then served in the Mediterranean and the Far East, and in 1945 she became one of the first submarines to be fitted with a schnorkel. She was wrecked while on her way to the breakers in December 1946.

**▼70**

**71.** HMS *Tantivy*, seen here on 17 April 1945 arriving at Fort Blockhouse from the Far East, was one of sixteen 'T' class submarines built under the 1940 and War Emergency Programmes. From P.332 onwards all the boats were of welded construction, which enabled some of the ballast tanks to be converted to carry fuel, whilst several of the later boats were fitted with a 20mm Oerlikon in a bandstand aft of the conning tower. *Tantivy*, together with six others of this group, had the external bow tubes moved aft by 7ft to fine the shape of the bow and eliminate the noticeable bow wave caused by the bulge when the boat was running at periscope depth. *Tantivy* was built by Vickers in 1943 and expended as an asdic target in 1951. (IWM A.28238)

**72.** *Tempest* surfaces after enduring nearly seven hours of depth-charging by the Italian torpedo boat *Circe* on 13 February 1942. *Tempest* had been detected by *Circe* while the latter was hunting for HMS *Una*, which had just torpedoed an Italian tanker. There were 24 survivors from the British submarine's complement of 63. (IWM HU.2278)

▲ 73

▲ 74    ▼ 75

**73.** The 4in Mk. XII gun on board HMS *Taurus*. The gun fired a 35lb shell to a maximum range of 1,040yds at 20 degrees of elevation. The S.1 hand-worked mounting allowed +20 to −3 degrees of elevation and the rate of fire was 12 rounds per minute. (IWM A.21521)

**74.** *Traveller*, built in 1941 by Scotts and photographed here on contractor's trials on 27 March 1942 in the Gareloch. She was not fitted with a 20mm Oerlikon. Note how the two midships external torpedo tubes have been fitted to fire aft and 'coned' to give the distinctive broad after casing; note also the single external tube fitted in the after casing. In January 1943 *Traveller* was reported 'overdue and presumed lost': she had probably been mined early in December 1942 while engaged in a reconnaissance of the approaches to Taranto harbour. (IWM A.9822)

**75.** *Turbulent*'s crew display a 'Jolly Roger' covered with symbols indicating successes against Axis targets. This boat was under the command of Cdr. J. 'Tubby' Linton, who was posthumously awarded the Victoria Cross, not for one particular event but for the aggressive and relentless way in which he fought the enemy. Linton sank over 100,000 tons of enemy shipping, including the Italian destroyer *Pessagno*, and his score also included three trains shot up with gunfire. *Turbulent* was lost, probably mined, off Corsica in March 1943; during her last year of service she had been hunted thirteen times and been on the receiving end of over 250 depth charges. (IWM A.14794)

**76.** HMS *Tally-Ho* passes through the Great Bitter Lake: as with the 'S' Class, once submarine operations in the Mediterranean had been ended following the armistice with Italy, all new-construction 'T' Class boats were ordered to the Far East. *Tally-Ho*, one of five boats of the 1940 Programme to have their ballast tanks modified to carry another 86 tons of oil fuel, more than lived up to her nickname of the 'Hunting Submarine' by sinking the Japanese light cruiser *Kuma* on 11 January 1944 off Penang and evading the subsequent depth charge attack by steering towards the shore. This success was following on 14 February by the sinking of the German submarine *UIT-23*, the former Italian *Reginaldo Giulani*. (IWM A.31033)

**77.** An interesting encounter for *Tally-Ho* came on the night of 24 February 1944, when a Japanese escort was sighted at close range – too close for the submarine to dive. The two ships met practically head on, and as the escort passed down *Tally-Ho*'s port side her propeller gouged out great lumps from the submarine's saddle tank. With the boat safely back in Ceylon, the damage was a source of wonder to many – 'just like a ruddy toast rack', commented one officer. (IWM A.22887)

76▲    77▼

 78

**78.** HMS *Thule*, built in 1942 at Portsmouth Dockyard, was one of the last group of 22 'T' Class submarines ordered under the 1941/42 Programmes; another five were cancelled while under construction. They differed little from the earlier boats except that they were fitted with air conditioning and improved radar. *Thule* was commanded by Lt. Cdr. Alistair Mars, who had commanded *Unbroken* (see below) in the Mediterranean. *Thule* was broken up in 1962. (IWM A.24334)

▼ 79

**79.** *Totem* under way on completion in 1944. Built at Devonport Dockyard in 1943, this boat was renamed *Dakar* and transferred to the Israeli Navy in 1964 but was lost, cause unknown, while on passage out to her new owners. Legend had it that should the totem pole presented to the submarine on commissioning be removed, then bad luck would befall the boat; the pole was indeed removed when the submarine was transferred to Israel (and is now in the RN Submarine Museum at Gosport). (IWM A.29867)

80▲

**80.** HMS *Trenchant* returns to Fremantle in Western Australia after a patrol in which, under the command of Cdr. A. R. Hezlet RN, she sank the 10,000-ton Japanese cruiser *Asigara* in a determined attack in the Banka Strait on 8 June 1945. After hitting *Asigara* with five out of eight torpedoes Hezlet permitted a 'periscope liberty', and some thirty members of *Trenchant*'s crew were able to see their target slowly sinking in what was Britain's last major submarine success of the Second World War. Note the camouflage scheme: light colours protected the submarine at night at night while darker ones concealed her during the day. (IWM A.30366)

**81.** A fine view of *Trenchant*'s conning tower, showing both periscope standards (with the attack periscope raised), the Type 291 radar aerial and the Oerlikon gun with its safety rail designed to prevent an over-enthusiastic gunner from removing the tops of the periscopes! (IWM ABS.434)

81▼

▲82

**82.** *Tireless* under way off Spithead on 28 May 1945. Note how the fining of the bow makes the external forward tubes more visible. *Tireless* was built at Portsmouth Dockyard in 1943 and broken up in 1968. (IWM A.2928)

**83.** *Tireless* was one of the last of the 'T' Class to be completed, and in the 1950s was selected for streamlining to improve underwater performance and reduce noise. This involved the removal of all external torpedo tubes except the single stern tube, rebuilding the casing, and enclosing the masts and periscopes in a 'fin'. Four other 'T' Class submarines were similarly converted. This photograph shows *Tireless* in August 1952. (IWM FXL. 11292)

**84.** HMS *Tabard* in June 1955. A further eight boats of the 'T' Class underwent 'super' conversion, which involved lengthening the hull by some 20ft and installing another pair of electric motors, together with a fourth section of high-capacity batteries which increased the underwater speed to 15kts. *Tabard* remained in service until 1968. (IWM FXL.13556)

**85.** HMS *Undine*, launched in 1937 at Barrow, was the first of the 'U' Class submarines designed for training duties and as

replacements for the 'H' Class. They were originally to be unarmed but during their construction provision was made for four internal bow torpedo tubes together with two external tubes in the bulge above the bow. The hull was also strengthened forward of the conning tower so that a deck gun could be fitted. The 'Us' were of single-hull design, with all ballast and fuel tanks inside the pressure hull, and had a diving depth of 200ft. *Undine* was sunk, possibly at the hands of the German 1st Minesweeping Flotilla, on 7 January 1940.

**86.** *Ursula*, also built by Vickers, was another of the early 'U' class boats. The two external bow tubes are clearly visible in this photograph – only the first three boats of the class were so completed. Surface propulsion was diesel-electric, the two Paxman Ricardo 615bhp diesels being connected directly to two generators which supplied power to two 825shp motors driving the propellers; for submerged running the submarine was powered by two sets of storage batteries. *Ursula* was handed over to the USSR in 1944 and redesignated *B4*. She was returned to Britain in 1949 and broken up shortly afterwards. (Author's Collection)

▼83

84▲

85▲   86▼

▲87

**87.** *Una*, seen here at Malta on 13 February 1943, was one of only two 'U' Class boats of the 1940/41 Programme to be built at Chatham Dockyard (the other was *Umpire*); the remaining 44 were all built by Vickers. Note the flat shape of the bow compared with *Undine* and *Ursula*. All the units of the 1940/41 Programme had the bow external tubes removed and the bow lengthened and flattened, in order to remove the noticeable wave caused by the bulge when the submarine was running at periscope depth. *Upholder, Unique, Upright, Usk, Utmost* and *Unbeaten*, however, were completed with the raised bow but without external tubes. *Una* was broken up at Llanelly in 1949. (IWM A.14527)

**88.** Two 'U' Class submarines at Malta in March/April 1943: in the foreground is HMS *Unison* and behind her is *Unseen*. The small dimensions of the 'U' Class (191ft overall × 16ft) gave them excellent handling qualities and their equipment was simple and rational, resulting in a high degree of operational reliability. They were much smaller than contemporary boats of foreign navies, and some aspects of their design were clearly the result of wartime austerity, but their shortcomings were more than offset by the large numbers constructed – 49 hulls in all. (IWM A.16265)

▼88

**89.** The 3in gun on board HMS *Unseen* at Malta in March–April 1943. Early boats of the class had a 12pdr gun but later boats were fitted with the 3in weapon, which fired a 17.5lb shell to a range of 12,920yds at 40 degrees elevation. (IWM A.16269)

**90.** HMS *Unruly*, built in 1942, enters Algiers harbour, April 1943. The 'U' Class served with great distinction in the Mediterranean, where their small size was an asset, but losses were high – thirteen boats of the class were casualties in this theatre. (IWM A.16887)

▲ 91

**91.** Lt. Cdr. M. D. Wanklyn (centre), commanding officer of HMS *Upholder*, with some of his ship's company at Malta. Wanklyn had been awarded the Victoria Cross for a determined and skilfully executed attack on the Italian liner *Conte Rosso* on 24 May 1941, and his total 'score' included over 100,000 tons of enemy merchant shipping, the Italian submarines *Tricheco* and *Ammiraglio St. Bon* and the Italian destroyer *Libeccio*. Wanklyn never lost an opportunity to attack the enemy. On the night of 12 April 1941 he sighted a southbound convoy of five merchant ships, and, having expended all his torpedoes, fired enough starshell from the deck gun to convince the Italians that an attack by British surface forces was imminent, with the result that the convoy returned to harbour. *Upholder* was sunk on 14 April 1942 north-west of Tripoli after a

savage depth charge attack by the Italian destroyer *Pegaso*. There were no survivors. (IWM A.7294)

**92.** HMS *Unbroken* returns to Portsmouth on 26 April 1943 after a successful deployment in the Mediterranean. In the summer of 19 *Unbroken* led the return of the 10th Submarine Flotilla to Malta an on 13 August 1942 scored a spectacular success by torpedoing two Italian cruisers west of Lipari Island. *Muzio Attendolo* lost 60ft of her bows and *Bolzano* was badly damaged. *Unbroken*'s other activities in the Mediterranean included destroying a southbound goods train in Calabria and blocking the main west coast railway li for 24 hours for the expenditure of ten rounds of 3in ammunition. (IWM A.18913)

▼ 92

**93▲**

**3.** HMS *Unruffled* at Malta in April 1943. On 8 December the previous year this submarine blew the bows off the Italian cruiser *Attilo Regolo* while on patrol off Cape St. Vito. *Unruffled* survived the war and was broken up at Troon in January 1946. (IWM A.14689)

**4.** A periscope photograph of the Italian merchant ship *Loretto* sinking on 13 October 1942 after being torpedoed by HMS *Unruffled* off Cape Gallo. The 'U' Class submarines operating in the Mediterranean took a heavy toll (sometimes as high as 50 per cent) of Rommel's supply ships and seriously interfered with German and Italian attempts to reinforce their armies in North Africa at the time of the Battle of El Alamein. (IWM AXA.139)

**94▼**

**95, 96.** HMS *Umbra* returns to Devonport, July 1943. Under the command of Lt. Maydon RN (photograph 96 shows him at *Umbra*'s periscope), this boat torpedoed and damaged the Italian battleship *Littorio* and sank the cruiser *Trento* in the same attack on 15 June 1942. Maydon was aiming for the battleship when aircraft of the RAF bombed the Italian ships, causing them to put their helms hard over. At long range Maydon fired a full salvo and scored one hit. He then noticed that the cruiser had stopped because of bomb damage and, after hurriedly reloading his torpedo tubes, finished her off. (IWM A.14962/IWM A.14964)

▲ 95    ▼ 96

**97.** A cheerful group of *Umbra*'s seamen display their 'Jolly Roger' on their return to Britain. Among *Umbra*'s successes was an Italian aircraft which was reportedly destroyed in the explosion of a torpedoed supply ship. (IWM A.14972)

**98.** HMS *Vortex*, built in 1944 by Vickers, was one of 22 'V' Class submarines, which were slightly longer and faster variants of the 'U' Class although they retained the same basic characteristics. The use of welding in their construction meant that the 'Vs' had a greater diving depth and were cheaper and quicker to build. On completion *Vortex* was transferred to the Free French naval forces and renamed *Morse*. She served with the French until 1947, when she was transferred to Denmark and renamed *Saelen*, being finally broken up in 1958. (IWM FXL.6777)

97▲                    98▼

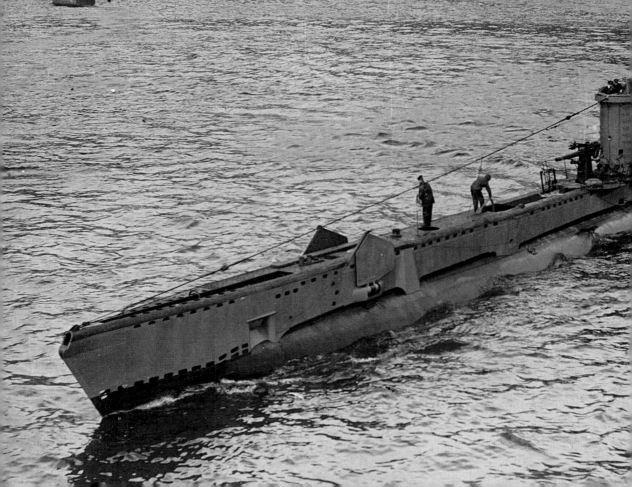

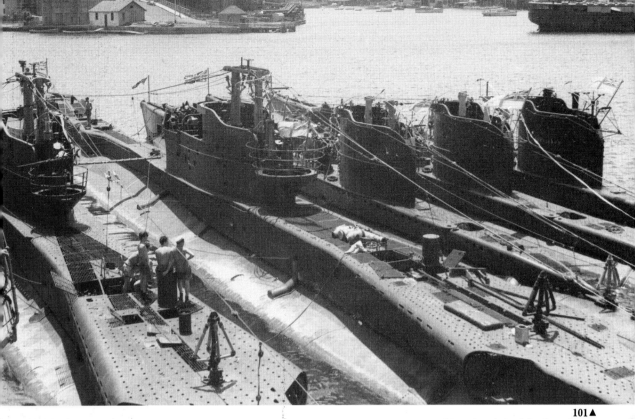

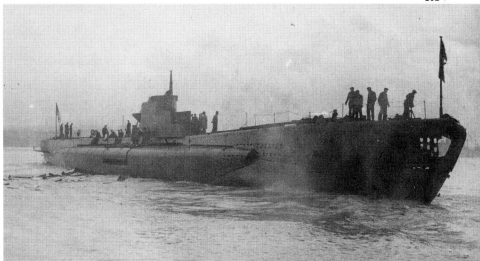

**99.** HMS *Vulpine* under way in Liverpool Bay on 13 October 1944 with a schnorkel unit in place of her after periscope. The schnorkel was in fact a dummy, the only purpose of which was to train RAF aircrew in tracking German U-boats equipped with the genuine article. *Vulpine* was built by Vickers in 1943 and broken up in 1959. (IWM A.25976)

**100.** *Venturer*, seen here in Holy Loch on 28 August 1943, was the first of the 'V' Class to be completed and distinguished herself by sinking two German U-boats, *U771* on 11 November 1944 and *U864* on 9 February 1945. The sinking of *U864* is a unique achievement in submarine history since both boats were submerged at the time of the attack and *Venturer*'s commanding officer, Lt. J. S. Launders RN, aimed his four torpedoes by asdic. On surfacing Launders found a large oil slick, wooden wreckage and a large metal cylinder – all that remained of *U864*. (IWM A.18832)

**101.** Three 'V' Class submarines alongside two 'T' Class boats at Sydney in the summer of 1945: (from right to left) HMS *Voracious*, *Vox* (ii), *Virtue*, *Taurus* and *Totem*. The majority of the 'V' Class served in home waters, but five were sent to the Pacific to assist in ASW training, their range being too limited for operational work. Note the shape of the single-hull 'V' Class compared with the saddle tank 'Ts'. (IWM ABS.1414)

**102.** The launch of HMS *Affray* at Cammell Laird's Birkenhead yard, 20 April 1945. The 'A' Class were the only British submarines to be designed during the Second World War, and the design incorporated many of the lessons learned from war experience. The 'As' were intended for operations in the Far East and so had the high surface speed of 18½kts, considerable endurance (10,500 miles at 11kts) and enhanced crew habitability. *Affray* was lost in the English Channel in April 1951, the cause being given as a break in the 'snort' induction tube. (IWM A.28191)

▲103

▲104 ▼105

**103.** *Auriga* on her completion in 1946. The 'A' Class were of double-hull construction and had a displacement of 1,385 tons surfaced and 1,620 tons submerged. *Auriga* was armed with six bow tubes (four internal, two external) and four stern tubes (two internal, two external) and could carry twenty reload torpedoes or alternatively 26 Mk. V mines. A 4in Mk. XXIII gun and a 20mm Oerlikon completed the armament. (IWM Fl.1206)

**104.** *Amphion* was the first of the 'A' Class submarines to be laid down, by Vickers, in November 1943. This photograph was taken on 15 February 1945 and shows her as completed, with the low bow and short periscope standards. Only *Amphion* and *Astute* were completed in this form: the low bow was found to give poor sea-keeping qualities and in the other boats of the class the bow was raised to allow a buoyancy tank to be incorporated. (IWM FL.614)

**105.** This fine 1955 photograph of *Astute* at Devonport shows clearly the effect of raising the bow; note also the increased height of the periscope standards. Type 138B asdic has been fitted on the casing

aft of the conning tower and the FM DF coil, together with the 20mm Oerlikon platform, has been removed. (IWM Fl.1148)

**106.** HMS *Anchorite* on completion, 18 November 1947. Built by Vickers at Barrow, this boat served with the Royal Navy until August 1970, when she was sold for breaking up. Note the raised mast for the Type 291 radar array. The 'As' were the first class of submarines of all-welded construction completed for the Royal Navy. Production times averaged eight months from keel-laying to launch, compared to 15 months for a 'T' Class boat. (IWM FL.533)

**107.** The conning tower of *Artful*, October 1952. *Artful* was the only boat of the class to be completed without any gun armament. Note the 'snort' exhaust fitted to the ANF radar mast and the 'snort' induction tube in the lowered position at the port side of the after casing. The induction tube was raised hydraulically and secured in position by a locking pin operated from the control room. Seven of the sixteen 'A' Class submarines were completed with a snort system and the rest were modified to take one. (IWM FL.1082)

**107 ▼**

▲108
**108.** This 1965 photograph shows *Artemis* after 'streamlining'.
Between 1955 and 1960 all the 'A' Class except *Aurochs* were taken
in hand for modernization work similar to that carried out on the 'T'
Class. All the remaining external torpedo tubes were removed and a
new lightweight casing fitted. The periscope standards and radar
masts were enclosed in a new 26½ft high 'fin', a combined
telescopic 'snort' and induction mast being fitted in the after end of
the fin of some boats. The buoyancy tank in the bow was removed
and the bow given a flatter profile, which greatly improved
underwater speed. (IWM FL.1056)

**109.** *Artemis* came to a sad end. On 1 July 1971, while alongside
the jetty at HMS *Dolphin*, the submarine sank while her tanks were
being 'first-filled' with water before refuelling. She lost her trim,
and water poured in through open hatches on the casing which
could not be closed because of power cables which connected the
submarine to the shore power supply. Three men were trapped in
the fore ends but escaped. Here the top of *Artemis*' fin can be seen
above the water in Haslar Creek alongside HMS *Ocelot*. (IWM
FL.3439)

▼109

**110 ▲**

**0.** HMS *Aeneas* on completion, July 1946. *Aeneas* and *Acheron*
[we]re the only boats of the class to be fitted with a twin 20mm
[O]erlikon gun, which can be seen in the photograph (*Acheron's* twin
[m]ounting was removed shortly after completion). Also visible are
[th]e raised masts for the ANF and Type 291 radars and the two
[ex]ternal after torpedo tubes. (IWM FL.211)

**[11]1.** In 1972 *Aeneas* was loaned to the Vickers group and fitted with

a mounting for the SLAM (Submarine Launched Airflight Missile),
similar to the Blowpipe system used by the Army. The retractable
launcher can be seen here in the raised position above its housing in
the forward part of the fin. Although the trials were a success the
weapon was not adopted by the RN and in November 1972 *Aeneas*
returned to Plymouth to pay off. (IWM FL.288)

**111 ▼**

▲ 112

**112.** HMS *Andrew*, built in 1946, was the only submarine of the class not to be fitted with a 20mm Oerlikon during her service. Another distinguishing feature of *Andrew* was the distinctive 4in gun shield – compare it with that fitted in *Astute* and *Anchorite*. (IWM FL.567)

**113.** Her casing party clad in local costume, *Andrew* moves away from the depot ship *Forth* at Singapore to return to the UK in September 1968. *Andrew* was the last of the 'A' Class to remain in service and was not broken up until May 1977. (IWM FL.657)

**114.** An interesting photograph of *Andrew*'s 4in Mk. XXIII gun on the S2 mounting being removed at HMS *Dolphin* after her last gun action in December 1974. Her commanding officer marked the

end of an era with a signal to FOSM: 'The reek of cordite has pass from the Royal Navy's submarine service. Last gun action conducted at 03 1330 Zulu. Time to 1st round – 36 seconds. May the art of submarine gunnery rest in peace but never be forgotten' (IWM FL.644)

**115.** (Next spread) HMS *Alliance* wearing an unusual camouflage scheme while on patrol in 1965 during the Indonesian confrontation. The folding 'snort' mast on the port side of the afte casing was later replaced by a combined snort/induction mast in th after part of the fin. *Alliance* is preserved today as a memorial at th Royal Navy Submarine Museum at Gosport.

114

▼ 113

▲ 116

**116.** No account of British submarines during the Second World War would be complete without a mention of the famous midget submarines or 'X-craft'. Thirty-two of these small submarines were built and served with great distinction in home waters and the Far East. Their principal weapon was two explosive charges which they attached to the hulls of enemy warships. Space precludes any description of their operations, but of the nine Victoria Crosses awarded to submariners during the Second World War, four were won in X-craft operations. This photograph shows *XT1*, a training submarine, under way in Holy Loch on 7 February 1944. (IWM A.21690)

**117.** The white ensign looks incongruous on the well-known silhouette of the Type VIIC U-boat. This photograph shows *U570* under new management as HMS *Graph*. Built in 1941 by Blohm und Voss, *U570* surrendered on 28 August 1941 and provided muc useful information on German submarine construction. *Graph* was wrecked off Islay in March 1944. (IWM A.9874)

▼ 117